Orange Tree Theatre

buckets

A NEW PLAY BY ADAM ~~~~~~~

GW00503759

Cast
JON FOSTER
TOM GILL
CHARLOTTE JOSEPHINE
SARAH MALIN
RONA MORISON
SOPHIE STEER

Community Ensemble **SHAILLA BAROK, HAZEL COLLINSON, DAVID CROFT, JANET DARE, BECKY FLISHER, LAURA HEPWORTH, MIRA IHASZ, JOYANNA LOVELOCK, JENNIFER MATTHEWS, ANGIE NEWMAN, PHOEBE RODRIGUES, IMOGEN ROUX, LOIS SAVILL, SAMANTHA SCOTT, DANIELLE THOMPSON, GRAHAM WILLIAMS**

Director **RANIA JUMAILY**
Designer **JAMES TURNER**
Lighting Designer **ELLIOT GRIGGS**
Musical Arrangements **CANDIDA CALDICOT**
Singing Supervisor **SUE APPLEBY**
Casting Consultant **VICKY RICHARDSON**

Production Manager **STUART BURGESS**
Deputy Stage Manager **SOPHIE ACREMAN**
Assistant Stage Managers **BECKY FLISHER, MICA TAYLOR**
Production Technician **TJ CHAPPELL**
Costume Supervisor **KATY MILLS**

Production Photographer **ROBERT DAY**

Orginially commissioned by **the egg**
Thanks to the **National Theatre Studio**

First performance at the Orange Tree Theatre 28 May 2015

Biographies

JON FOSTER

Theatre includes *All I Want* (Jackson's Lane/Newcastle Live);
Idomeneus, Trojan Women, Dream Story, Mud (Gate); *Cheese*
(fanSHEN); *A Beginning, A Middle and an End, Tenet* (Greyscale);
Invisible (Transport Theatre); *The Alchemist* (Firehouse Creative);
*A New Way to Please You, Sejanus: His Fall, Speaking Like
Magpies, Thomas Moore* (RSC); *How to Tell the Monsters
from the Misfits* (Birmingham Rep); *Long Time Dead* (Paines
Plough); *After Heggarty* (Finborough); *Food* (Traverse); *Dr Jekyll
and Mr Hyde* (Babayaga); *Free From Sorrow* (Living Pictures);
Romeo and Juliet (Creation); *Oliver Twist* (Instant Classics); *The
Melancholy Hussar* (Etcetera Theatre); *The Two Gentlemen of
Verona* (Pentameters); and *Treasure Island* (Palace Theatre).

TV includes *Da Vinci's Demons, The Great Fire, New Tricks,
Rev, The Smoke, Southcliffe, The Town, Mrs Biggs, Abroad,
Come Rain Come Shine, EastEnders, Love and Order, The
Bill, Clone, The IT Crowd, The Last Enemy, Instinct* and *Silent
Witness*.

Films include *Nice Guy* and *Love's Kitchen*.

TOM GILL

Tom trained at Guildford School of Acting.
Theatre credits include the Royal Shakespeare Company &
National Theatre of Scotland's UK and US tour of *Dunsinane,
Goodbye Barcelona* (Arcola); *Life On A Plum/Banging Wolves*
(Wilderness Festival) *Zig-Zag Zig-Zag* (Manchester International
Festival) *How We Won The World* (24:7 Festival) *Stomp*
(Theatre503) and *Territory* (Lowry).

Film work includes *Angels in Small Change* and *Eden Lake*.
Tom is also a Spoken Word Artist and the current UK Slam Poetry
Champion. He was winner of the Kate Tempest Lyrical Fireworks
award in association with Paines Plough and was recently
commissioned to do a piece for Channel 4. He has featured at
a range of venues and festivals across the UK including Ronnie
Scott's Jazz Club, Vault Festival & Tricycle Theatre.

CHARLOTTE JOSEPHINE

Charlotte trained on the Contemporary Theatre course at East
15 Acting School. She is co-artistic director of Snuff Box Theatre,
writing and performing award winning *Bitch Boxer* (Soho Theatre,
Edinburgh Festival, national and international tour). Charlotte is
currently writing for Soho Theatre's Soho Six programme. Other
theatre includes Secret Theatre at Lyric Hammersmith and *Julius
Caesar* at the Donmar Warehouse.

SARAH MALIN

Theatre work includes *The Cherry Orchard* (Young Vic); *Cuckoo* (Unicorn); *Unrivalled Landscape* (Orange Tree); *An Enemy of The People* (Just Jones); *Say it With Flowers* (Hampstead); *Blue Sky* (Hampstead and Pentabus); *Here Lies Mary Spindler* (RSC at Latitude); *Marianne Dreams* (Almeida); *The Penelopiad, Macbett, Macbeth* (RSC); *Iphigenia at Aulis* (National Theatre); *Pericles* (Lyric Hammersmith); *The Cherry Orchard* (English Touring Theatre); *The Norman Conquests* (Theatr Clwyd); *Ring* (Soho Theatre); *Dangerous Corner, Dead Wood* (Watermill, Newbury); *The Book of David* (Really Useful Group); *Grimm Tales* (Scarborough); *Twelfth Night* (Imaginary Forces); *The Tinderbox, World on Fire, David Copperfield* (New Vic, Stoke); *No Way Out* (ATC); *Madness in Valencia, Hecuba* (Gate); *The Merchant of Venice* (Sherman); *The Spanish Tragedy* (Old Red Lion); and *Blavatsky's Tower* (Red Room).

TV includes *What Remains, EastEnders, The Children, Wire in the Blood, Silent Witness, Guardian, The Knock, Emmerdale, The Law, The Bill* and *Every Silver Lining.*
Short films include *School Gates.*

RONA MORISON

Rona trained at Guildhall.

Theatre work includes *Scuttlers* (Royal Exchange Theatre); *The James Plays* (National Theatre/National Theatre of Scotland); *Anhedonia* (Royal Court); *To Kill a Mockingbird* (Open Air Theatre, Regent's Park); *Illusions* (Bush Theatre); *The Second Mrs Tanqueray* (Rose Theatre Kingston); and *Crave* (ATC).

Film includes *Love Bite, The Boy I Loved.*

SOPHIE STEER

Sophie trained at LAMDA. Her theatre work includes: Juliet in *Romeo and Juliet* (Watermill Theatre); *MilkMilkLemonade* (OvalHouse); *I Feel Fine* (New Diorama); *The Apple Cart* (FanSHEN at Latitude); *The Fitzrovia Radio Hour* tour; *All Good Men* (Finborough); *Sense* (Hen and Chickens); *Is Everyone Ok?* (Nabakov, Nu:Write Festival).

TV includes *Chickens* (Big Talk).

Short films include *Calibans Cave* (short film adaptation of Tim Crouch's 'I, Caliban'); *A Thousand Empty Glasses* (nominated for Best Short at Raindance/ Palm Springs Festivals).

ADAM BARNARD Writer

Adam Barnard began his career as a theatre director and now increasingly writes.

buckets is his first full-length play. Previous one-act plays include *Closer Scrutiny* (Orange Tree, 2014), *I.S.S.(Y)* (Wilderness Festival, 2013) and *Too Small To Be A Planet* (Company of Angels / Latitude, 2012). *Invisible*, a play for young performers, is at Theatre Royal Plymouth in July.

As a director, he has worked extensively at the Orange Tree (starting as a trainee director, 2003-4), and at Trafalgar Studios, the Finborough, Arcola, King's Head, Salisbury Playhouse, Stephen Joseph Theatre, Lichfield Garrick, Edinburgh Fringe, HighTide and in Copenhagen and Vienna.

Until 2013 he was joint director of Company of Angels, where he created the new writing programme The Commissioners and the digital theatre programme Virtual Empty Space, and wrote and directed four short films. Previously he was founding artistic director of Activated Image. He also works sporadically as a newspaper journalist.

RANIA JUMAILY Director

Rania is the Orange Tree's Resident Director. Her directing credits include: *My Twin* (Royal Court/Wilderness Festival); *Blues in the Night, Most Savage* and *Unnatural* (The Last Refuge),*Thermidor/All Good Men* (Finborough), *Wonderful Town* (Associate Director, Lowry/National Tour), *Oh What A Lovely War, Much Ado About Nothing* (Oval House), *The Threepenny Opera* (Lost Theatre), *Over the Moon* (New Wimbledon Studio), *First Lady Suite* (Union Theatre), and *The Bully Composition* (Southwark Playhouse)

Rania was Artistic Director of The Last Refuge and Company Associate at The Tank in New York.

JAMES TURNER Designer

Trained: Motley Theatre Design Course.

Recent designs include: *Cuddles* (59E59, New York/ Ovalhouse/UK Tour); *The Father* (Trafalgar Studios 2); *Donkey Heart* (Trafalgar Studios 2/Old Red Lion); *State Red* (Hampstead Theatre); *The Cherry Orchard Parallel Production* (Young Vic); *Honest* (Salisbury Playhouse/UK Tour); *Toast* (Park Theatre); *John Ferguson, A Life, The Sluts of Sutton Drive* (Finborough); *Mercury Fur* (Trafalgar Studios 2/Old Red Lion); *The Armour, The Hotel Plays* (Langham Hotel); *Our Ajax, I Am A Camera, Execution of Justice* (Southwark Playhouse); *MilkMilkLemonade*

(Oval House); *Goodnight Children Everywhere* (Drama Centre London); *The Suicide, Cause Célèbre* (CSSD); *Strong Arm, That Moment* (Underbelly, Edinburgh); *Thrill Me* (Charing Cross Theatre/Edinburgh Festival/UK Tour); *Plain Jane* (Royal Exchange Studio); *No Wonder* (Library Theatre); *A Man of No Importance* (Union Theatre/Arts Theatre).

Recent work as Associate Designer includes: *A View from the Bridge* (Wyndham's Theatre/Young Vic); *An Intervention* (Watford Palace/Paines Plough); *Jumpers for Goalposts* (Bush Theatre/Paines Plough).

Awards: Best Set Designer (Off West End Awards 2013)

ELLIOT GRIGGS Lighting Designer
Elliot trained at RADA.

Recent lighting designs include: *Hansel and Gretel* (Belgrade Theatre Coventry); *Deluge* (Hampstead Theatre); *Lampedusa* (Soho Theatre/HighTide Festival/Unity Theatre, Liverpool); Contact (Bravo 22); *Yen* (Royal Exchange); *Benefit* (Cardboard Citizens); *Pomona* (Orange Tree); *Fleabag* (Soho Theatre/ UK Tour); *Henry IV* (Associate Lighting Designer, Donmar Warehouse); *CommonWealth* (Almeida Theatre); *Defect* (Perfect Pitch/Arts Ed); *He Had Hairy Hands, The Boy Who Kicked Pigs* (The Lowry, Manchester/UK tour); *Marching On Together* (Old Red Lion); *Rachel, John Ferguson, Spokesong, The Soft of her Palm, And I* and *Silence* (Finborough Theatre); *Infanticide* (Camden People's Theatre); *Belleville Rendez-Vous* (Greenwich Theatre); *Meat* (Theatre503); *Lagan* (Oval House Theatre); *Love Re:Imagined* (Only Connect); *Folk Contraption* (Southbank Centre).

Awards: Best Lighting Designer (Off West End Awards 2014); New Talent in Entertainment Lighting (Association of Lighting Designers 2014); Francis Reid Award (Association of Lighting Designers 2011); ShowLight Award (NSDF 2009).

CANDIDA CALDICOT Musical Arrangements
Candida is also currently the Musical Director on J.M Barrie's *Peter Pan* (Regent's Park Open Air Theatre)

Other theatre as Musical Director: *A Mad World My Masters* (English Touring Theatre); *The Witch of Edmonton, The Heresy of Love, The Heart of Robin Hood, The Tempest* (RSC); *The Tempest* (RSC US Suitcase Tour); *Galileo* (Birmingham Rep); *A Soldier in Every Son* (International Tour); *Bed and Sofa* (Finborough); *The Vaudevillians* (Lowry and Charing Cross); *Everything Must Go* (Soho).

Other theatre includes: *The White Devil, Arden of Faversham, Titus Andronicus, Richard III, King John, City Madam, Wendy and Peter, 50 years of the RSC Musical* (RSC); *The Sound of Music, The Wizard of Oz* (Palladium); *La Cage Aux Folles* (Playhouse).

Composing: Promenade Summer Seasons 2009-2014 (Iris Theatre); *Macbeth* (Shakespeare in Styria); *Once Upon a Time* (Booktrust Tour); *The Hostage* (Southwark Playhouse); *Currently Orchestrating Prodigy* (St James).

SUE APPLEBY Singing Supervisor

Sue has been an actress, singer and musical director for nearly 15 years. In this time she has played in over 25 countries, at the National Theatre, Royal Albert Hall and London's West End on several occasions. She trained at The Central School of Speech and Drama and the University of Birmingham, and has a first class degree in Music and Drama.

Sue sings regularly with the Maida Vale Singers and has worked with conductor John Wilson and his Orchestra in The Good Companions for Radio 3, the Rodgers and Hammerstein and Hollywood Proms for BBC TV/Radio 3 and at Abbey Road Studios.

Her work as musical director includes *Three Men in a Boat, 20,000 Leagues Under the Sea* alongside director John Godber, and the West End productions of *Cool Hand Luke* (Aldwych), *Carrie's War* (Apollo), *Little Women* (Duchess) and *Anne of Green Gables* (Lilian Baylis). She coaches singing for many industry professionals, with her company London Singing Works, as well as teaching singing at two of London's top drama schools. www.sueappleby.co.uk

Photos of the cast in rehearsal by Robert Day
From top left: Jon Foster, Tom Gill, Charlotte Josephine,
Sarah Malin, Rona Morison, Sophie Steer

Orange Tree Theatre

We aim to stir, delight, challenge, move and amaze with a bold and continually evolving mix of new and re-discovered plays in our unique in-the-round space. We want to change lives by telling remarkable stories from a wide variety of times and places, filtered through the singular imagination of our writers and the remarkable close-up presence of our actors.

A theatre of this scale, with the audience wrapped around the players, invites acting to be the centre of the experience. This is theatre as a figurative art: the human being literally at its centre. We want to experience voices and stories from our past and our present alongside visions of the future. Life as it's lived: unplugged and un-miked. Close-up magic. Truths the hand can touch.

Over its 42-year history the Orange Tree has had a very strong track record in discovering writers and promoting their early work, as well re-discovering artists from the past whose work had either been disregarded or forgotten. Martin Crimp, James Saunders, Vaclav Havel, Fay Weldon and Torben Betts were championed at early stages of their development, and the reputations of Rodney Ackland, Harley Granville Barker, Susan Glaspell, John Whiting and Githa Sowerby have undergone radical re-assessment after seasons of their work at the Orange Tree.

Play Your Part
Become a Member

Why support us

You know that at the Orange Tree we make great theatre in a very special setting. To do that requires the skill and talent of a great many actors, writers, designers and directors, not to mention our incredible team backstage. But crucially it also relies on your support.

Without committed supporters like you, we wouldn't have the resources to stage such a variety of work and to such a high standard. Since April 2015 we no longer receive regular funding from the Arts Council. Signing up for an Orange Tree membership means that you will be helping to secure our future and enable us to go on flourishing.

The best seats in the house

Our acclaimed productions regularly sell out, and being able to secure the seat you want in advance with priority booking means you'll never miss a show again. As well as that, a variety of exclusive events are laid on for Members throughout the year, giving you a unique insight into our work.

Memberships start at just £30, and our different levels give you access to all our shows and the creative processes behind them.

You can join in person at the Box Office, online via orangetreetheatre.co.uk or over the phone on 020 8940 3633.

Join now and play your part!

Thank you

Paul Miller
Artistic Director

Staff

Artistic Director **Paul Miller**
Executive Director **Sarah Nicholson**
Development Director **Alex Jones**
Front of House Manager **Derek Lamden**
Box Office Manager **Hayley Williams**
Financial Controller **Bhamini Jebanesan**
Office Manager **Rebecca Murphy**
Press & Marketing Manager **Ben Clare**
Community & Education Director **Imogen Bond**
Outreach, Education & Youth Theatre Co-ordinator **Corinne Meredith**
Memberships Officer **Nick Bagge**
Literary Associate **Guy Jones**
Resident Director **Rania Jumaily**
Channel 4 Playwright **Melissa Bubnic**
Box Office Assistants **David Andrews, Kate Morrison-Wynne**
Production Manager **Stuart Burgess**
Stage Management Team **Sophie Acreman, TJ Chappell, Becky Flisher**
Resident Assistant Design **Katy Mills**
Youth Theatre Leaders **Sophie Boyce, Kate Morrison-Wynne,
Spencer Noll, Nadia Papachronopoulou, Karima Setohy,
Kenton Jordan Thomas**
House Managers **Brenda Newman, Angelica Wilson**
Bar Staff **Louise Collins, Grace Lightman, Alex Lightman,
J R May, Emily Moitoi-Sturman, Helen Peatfield, Corran Royle
Angelica Wilson, Imogen Watson**
Audio Describer **Veronika Hyks**

With thanks to **Rachel Middlemore** and **Katherine Ronayne**
The Orange Tree would like to thank all our ushers and volunteers

Associate Artists **David Antrobus, Carolyn Backhouse, Geoffrey Beevers,
Edward Bennett, Vincent Brimble, Anthony Clark, Steven Elder, Oliver Ford
Davies, Stuart Fox, Clive Francis, Vivien Heilbron, David Lewis, Christopher
Naylor, Amy Neilson Smith, Isobil Nisbet, Diana Payan, Amanda Royle, Auriol
Smith, Caroline Smith, Paula Stockbridge, Gillian Thorpe, Stephanie Turner,
Matthew Walters, Sam Walters, Timothy Watson, David Whitworth**

Board Members **Rodney Carran, Anthony Clark, Judith Coke, Steven Elder,
Kate Ellis** (vice chair), **Oliver Ford Davies, Nigel Hall, Richard Humphreys** (chair),
Vivien Heilbron, John Hudson, Ray Warner

This Theatre has the support of the Channel 4 Playwrights' Scheme sponsored by
Channel 4 Television

The Resident Director Scheme is supported by the Barbara Whatmore Charitable Trust,
Fenton Arts Trust and The Bulldog Prinsep Theatrical Fund

Richmond Parish Lands Charity, Hampton Fuel Allotment Charity and The Barnes
Workhouse Fund are supporters of our community and education programmes.

With thanks to Theatre Record.

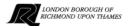

LONDON BOROUGH OF
RICHMOND UPON THAMES

buckets

Adam Barnard

Development of this play has been supported by the 2014 Leverhulme Arts Scholarship in association with the egg, Theatre Royal Bath; by the Orange Tree Theatre; and by the National Theatre Studio.

Thanks

The Leverhulme Trust and fellow 2014 Scholars, and all at the egg, especially Kate Cross, Katherine Lazare and Lee Lyford; all at the Orange Tree, especially Guy Jones, Paul Miller and Sarah Nicholson; the National Theatre Studio, especially Julia Thomas and Rachel Twigg; Nick Quinn.

The Devey family. Suzy Harvey. Dr Terry Matthews. Julia Woolley.

Various kind readers: Antony Antunes, Steven Bloomer, Hannah Boyde, Andrew Butler, Sophie Crawford, Nia Davies, Christopher Dickins, Nicholas Hart, Abigail Matthews, Jordan Mifsúd, Mark Oosterveen, Rebecca Pownall, Tara Robinson, Caitlin Shannon, Lisa Stevenson.

Sam Walters and Auriol Smith, for many things.

Rania for taking it to heart.

Margaret. William. Kelly.

For your very own limited-edition bonus scene from the *buckets* B-sides collection, apply to thatguywrotebuckets@gmail.com

In loving memory of Rebecca Vassie

4

Note on Text

buckets *can be performed by any number and composition of actors.*

Gender, where referenced in dialogue, can generally be switched – 'he' for 'she', 'mother' for 'father', etc. Some singular voices could be made plural – 'we' for 'I', etc.

A line that's just an ellipsis (…) is a moment where a speaker:

i) wants to communicate but can't, or
ii) communicates without words, or
iii) refuses to communicate, or
iv) is otherwise occupied

Where a line ends without punctuation, a choice should be made.

A new paragraph usually indicates a change of speaker.

Everything's an option.

This text went to press before the end of rehearsals and so may differ slightly from the play as performed.

DRAMA

8

1. Doctor

Of course it's up to you.

It's up to me.

It's your decision. It has to be.

I don't know how to decide.

There are different schools of thought. About how clearly a child this age can understand the idea of – the concept of – their own death. About whether to know, is to add depression and anxiety to an existing suffering. Whereas some judge that the best thing, the right thing, is simple honesty.

You're very – patient. You explain things well.

Thank you.

I've always meant to ask. Is that your daughter?

No. No it's my girlfriend. My partner.

Oh.

It's quite an old photo.

I never thought things were going to – nobody does, I suppose – when I think back to when I found out I was – I just couldn't have imagined that having a child would be – I don't know – oncology wards platelet counts nasogastric intubation vomit trays

I won't pretend that anyone can really imagine what all this is like for you.

When he was three we were out for a walk and we found a bird all splatted on the pavement, it must have dropped out of the sky, you can imagine, its insides oozing over its wings. I tried to distract him steer him away but too late. He was, he was entranced. He looked at it and he said 'It did all the things it wanted to, so it let its wings rest. Because flying's hard Mummy.' That's – I mean not every three-year-old comes out with stuff like that, do they?

You know your child better than anyone.

The thing is, I think he could handle it. I'm just not sure I could. I'm not sure I could sit there and tell him. I'm not sure I could carry on, him and me, knowing that he knows, with it all out in the open. I think I'd find it easier to continue as we've been.

Of course things won't be quite the same. We won't be doing the same level of testing. Because we're stopping treatment, he may have a brief upsurge. Where he has more energy and some of the symptoms that relate to the treatment – the vomiting, the diarrhoea, to an extent the tiredness – these things may actually get better, for a while. What you have therefore is a window, between the easing-off of these symptoms and the overall decline of his health. And this window might be a time to – if there are particular things he's always wanted to do. Or that you've wanted to do together.

We have we did a

Yes.

But – it was all things we'd do when he got better. You know, climb Mount Everest walk to the South Pole see the penguins fly on a commercial spaceship. We're not going to be able to do any of those things, are we?

Most people don't manage to do those things even if they're healthy. Even if they live to a hundred.

…

The danger in not telling him is he may get the impression, now that he is home more of the time and starting to feel better, that he is actually recovering. Which may demotivate him from doing things for which limited time remains.

It's been such a long road, hasn't it?

It has.

So many times I've sat in this… I feel like I've seen more of
you these last few years than anyone. Anyone adult I mean.
Well no not seen but – had a greater number of meaningful
moments. I feel, in a strange way, that I'm going to miss you.
Miss being here. That's strange isn't it?

I think it's normal. If it's useful I could recommend you, there's
this

Will you come to the. To the. Will you come to the

Yes. If you want me to be there.

And yet at some level I hate you.

Well, I

You are so calm. You show no emotion when you deliver
information that hits me like a train, like a high-speed train and
you're just. So. Smug. So – certain. Of medical facts. Of
probable outcomes. Of what you know and who you are and
what you do and why you do it. Because you grew up in time.
Didn't you. You got it right. When you were seventeen. Sixteen.
Younger. The choices you made. The exams you sat. That
decision to do something so very hard but so very rewarding.
You've set yourself up, and I'm not saying it was easy but now
you're all charged up and your whole life's running on its own.
And one day you'll look back and say, Yes. I did okay. But I, I,
I. I don't believe you need your glasses I think they are a prop.
Your girlfriend is too young. Your shoes are too shiny. You have
too many pens. You're just so obviously

No I understand, I do, I

Oh god I'm sorry. Why did I do that? I feel sick. I'm so sorry. I
wish I

2. Forward Planning

This is what it comes down to. I love you. And I think you're the one.

Yes.

I think we should be together all our lives.

Like we've talked about.

Like we've talked about, yes. I think we should do it all and do it first, before everyone else. Get married first, have kids first, baby one nine months after our honeymoon, okay maybe ten maybe eleven but within I don't know three, three-and-a-half years even allowing some months for slack we have a family, boom, created, so by the time we're I don't know forty, ish, our kids are pretty much grown up and we'll never be crap parents so much older than our kids that we don't get them and they hate us. By then we have some money and we can travel the world then be retired with a house in Spain or France or, with a pool and chickens for fresh eggs and a shed to paint in and an allotment to plant vegetables we'll grow and eat. We'll have grandkids who'll visit us and we'll be the coolest grandparents ever, young and up for everything and we'll be healthy in the sunshine and live really long and not work ourselves to death then cop it a year after retiring at sixty-seven because all we'll do for the next – twenty years, is save, work hard and save and bring up decent kids, while everyone else is frittering it away on things that don't matter, one more overpriced drink or crap package holiday or a new phone even though they had the last one two weeks ago. And I think you're the one to do these things with I really do. This is our dream we dreamed it together.

Yes.

But. You're only the third you know only the third person I've seen naked, well no not seen but intentionally been even part-naked with or and well only the second person actually that I've, that I've

I know

You know

And you're my

I know. And what worries me is, is this enough? To sustain us. To stop us being curious at thirty, forty, fifty when we're still, you know, still. And we don't want to be the kind of people that cheat in a marriage. And we don't want ours to be the kind of marriage where everyone says Oh they've done it too young and then it all goes wrong and everyone's all smug because they've been proved right. So. It just seems better to do it now. Before we're. You too, if you want. If there's still stuff you need to – what I'm saying is, I won't mind.

3. Pet Project

You look sad. Why are you sad?

My hamster's dying.

Is it?

It's a he.

Is he?

Yes.

That is sad.

I know.

What's wrong with him?

Well the life expectancy is one to three years and it's nearly three years now since I got him.

That doesn't make him dying. Unless he's actually ill with something.

I don't think he's ill.

Then but that's like saying all old people are dying just because they're close to the human life expectancy.

Well they are.

My grandmother's old but she's not dying.

If you say so.

Mind you, I should call her more.

Exactly. That's how I feel.

That you should

Because there's a lot of stuff my hamster's never experienced. And I've been thinking. You know. He's been a good pet. And he's lived a pretty sheltered life. And I think it would make him happy if he gets to experience a few of these things before he dies.

What sort of things?

Well he's never been to Alton Towers.

That's because he's a hamster.

That shouldn't be a barrier to access. Places like Alton Towers are all about accessibility these days, I mean they wouldn't dare, I'd go to the press or. Because all he's ever known is that one little spinning wheel but he definitely loves it and so imagine how he'd feel on a proper Ferris wheel? Or anyway also I was thinking maybe karaoke.

Right, because

He wouldn't sing. Obviously. But then not everyone who goes into the booth sings. Usually some people hog the mic most of the time and others are happy to hang back and let them do the singing.

But

And he's definitely going skydiving.

Skydiving

Absolutely.

Do you want to give him experiences or speed up his death?

I know him. He'll love it.

He'll probably have a heart attack.

Well then it's a beautiful way to go. What a fantastic final experience, to be hurtling towards the earth at terminal velocity.

(At what?)

That's how I'd like to go. Anyway it's all booked.

It's booked, you've

Confirmed this morning.

How exactly does a hamster skydive?

Same way we do. Just a smaller parachute.

You're going to throw your pet hamster out of a plane

Yes. No of course not. Come on. I'm joking.

Oh.

He'll be in my pocket.

Right.

Kind of strapped in with his head poking out. He can't wait.

Sorry but – what makes you think your hamster wants to do any of this?

No, it is, it's a fair question.

Yes.

Promise not to tell?

Okay.

I read his diary.

4. Free Time

We could go to the park.

No.

Ride our bikes.

No.

Go for a walk?

…

Shall we just watch TV then?

There's nothing on.

We could see a movie.

I've seen all the good ones.

Shall I put some music on?

…

While we decide.

I've got a headache.

Come on, let's go to the park.

I hate the park.

Are you sure you don't want to play again?

…

Play a different game?

…

Let's eat something.

I'm not hungry.

We could get an ice cream. Or something to drink. How about a milkshake one of those malt ones they do at that place you know where they mix in chocolate bars and it comes in a huge metal

I feel sick.

Oh! There's that thing you know at the community centre with the giant statues.

God.

Well what do you want to do?

I don't know. I don't know I don't know I don't know I don't know I don't know.

Don't get angry.

We're wasting time. We finally have some time and we're wasting it.

Well then let's do something.

WHAT THOUGH?

I don't know you don't want to do anything I suggest.

We didn't plan anything. We should have planned something. We should have planned something and we didn't.

It doesn't matter we just need to pick something now that we can do.

It's too late. It's too late to do anything good. It's too late. It's too late.

5. You're Going to Die

Why are you crying? What's the matter?

It's too awful.

What is?

It's terrible.

What's happened?

I'm so sorry.

What? Tell me.

You're going to die.

Well. Not immediately I hope.

And I'm going to die.

Yes. One day. Yes. You are going to die. We both are.

And it's just so awful. It's just so sad. I don't see how anyone can live, knowing what's going to happen.

6. Kiss Me 1 (The Mission)

Would you kiss me?

What?

Would you. Kiss me.

You mean, hypothetically?

Okay, hypothetically.

Hypothetically, would I kiss you?

Yes.

I don't know.

Okay.

I mean you're not bad looking.

Okay.

And you seem, kind of interesting.

Okay.

But I'd want to know more about you. Or at least have a stronger sense of who you are. I'd need you to have made me feel something.

I'm dying.

Oh come on.

No I am definitely going to die soon.

No, that's too

It's true. It's not a line

Does this often work has it worked before?

I've never tried it before, I only just

I'm going to go over there. Okay?

Can I come with you?

Bye.

7. Journalism

'A Cruel, Uncaring or Absent God – The Indefensible Suffering of a Terminally Ill Child'.

It's maybe a little long, for a headline.

I mean the piece is beautiful.

Thank you.

It's articulate it's honest it's specific it's moving it flows it disarms you it's even funny in a couple of places and at the end I was genuinely brushing away tears.

Right.

But it's not what I asked for.

I just thought maybe, when you saw it done this way

I wonder if you're doing this just to spite me

I'm not I

Just to make a point.

…

What we want – and you know this, but I'll say it again – what we need is lists. People like lists. They share lists. And when they see lists, in their Facebook feed or whatever, they click. They come to our page, we show them adverts, we get paid. That's it. That's the whole equation.

It's just so

'Ten Things I Learnt From A Dying Girl – Number Seven Will Change Your Life'. Then rewrite the copy as a list, one strapline for each point then two, three pars underneath, plus images of course or least some pretty credible suggestions, an animated GIF somewhere if you can, and make number seven something about living for the moment, do it now because tomorrow might not come, it's not the number of breaths you took it's the moments that took your breath away. Kind of thing.

But she didn't say any of that.

She doesn't have to have said it. It's not just about her. Put yourself in the story. What did you learn from her?

I didn't learn anything from her. She hasn't changed my life. She barely spoke – she can barely speak – she's not stupid but with all the drugs and the pain she can barely think straight let alone form lucid cogent arguments about the meaning of existence, and I mean she's just not sharp, mentally, she's hardly had a day's schooling in years.

What about serenity then? The inner calm you can find in the face of immense suffering – whatever experiences life deals you, you can take it well you can take it badly

She's not serene. She twists in pain. She grimaces. She cries. She's moody, uncommunicative, fidgety

Acceptance? Knowing that death is inevitable for all of us sooner or later?

She doesn't accept it. She thinks it isn't fair. She's dying far too early and she knows it.

Well help me out here. Find a different list.

I could break the illness into ten stages?

What about a bucket list? Every dying child has a bucket list right? 'This List of Ten Things Cancer Girl Melly Wants To Do Before She Dies Will Make You – '

She's not called Melly.

'Names have been changed', don't use her real

And she only has one thing on her list – she wants to get better.

Melly's a good name.

…Okay I could deal with the things I didn't know about childhood illness. About paediatric care, the difficulty of getting the right diagnosis, life in a children's ward –

Things that made you angry. Things that aren't right.

The lottery when it comes to which drugs you can access – which trials you can be part of.

'Thirteen Shocking Things I Learnt…

Okay

'…When I Made Friends With a Dying Girl'

Made friends.

'Number Six Will Make You Want to Start a Revolution.'

I hate it. But I'll do it.

Good. Decision. First thing tomorrow?

Right.

How's your daughter?

Fine.

Handful?

Not really.

You should come for dinner. Both of you.

…

I'm on your side you know.

I know.

You have to accept the world as it is. Play the hand you're given.

8. Being There

Did you see what happened?

What? Where?

Didn't you see it?

What?

Oh my god.

Did you film it?

No. Oh my god. I've got to speak to someone who was there.

9. Minecraft

I don't get it why do you do this?

I like it.

What's the point? How do you win?

You don't win. You just build stuff.

But how does it end?

There isn't an end.

Then what's the point?

It's fun.

Games are meant to have a purpose. A goal. It's competition. You compete against other people or against the game or against yourself even but the point is you either win or lose. You achieve the object, or you die trying. This is stupid. There's nothing to play for.

You don't get it.

You're right I don't get it.

…

What's that for?

You use it for moving soil or water or lava or milk.

I suppose it's a bit like building sandcastles.

It's nothing like that.

But that has an end. It ends when you leave the beach, or when the water comes up and washes them away.

10. Charity

I'm collecting for kids with cancer.

My friend has cancer.

I'm sorry to hear that

So can I have some of that money? For my friend?

It doesn't work like that I'm afraid.

What's the money for then?

Well, we're a professional charity, so it goes into a central pot and

Hi I'm collecting for my friend, he's got cancer.

Sorry, you can't –

I don't have a collection thingy but you can put it in my hat.

Excuse me, sorry, this is

He's in that hospital there. Do you see? One two three windows up, two along I think, you can sort of see a plant on the window sill. His mum got him that he hates it. I just want to buy him a decent meal. The food's – And a milkshake. He really likes milkshakes. Thank you. Thank you you're really kind.

Are you going to buy him a – milkshake now?

I think I'll stay here for a bit. I quite like this.

11. Stan

Hey do you like hip hop?

What?

Do you like hip hop?

Yeah.

Listen to this listen to this.

…

Yeah? Yeah?

It's alright.

It's wicked. Have you heard it before?

No.

It's not released yet. Do you like Eminem?

…

I love Eminem. Have you go his early stuff? Have you got *Infinite*?

I've heard it.

That stuff is bad. Oh wait here listen this is so classic. This bit. Here. Wait wait wait and 'You better lose yourself in the music the moment you own it you better never let it go you only get one shot do not miss your chance to blow this opportunity comes once in a lifetime' yeah?

...

If I could meet him that would be

Just kind of reading here so

That would be the greatest moment, the greatest

Kind of just want to read this, yeah?

But I'd be so scared too. What if something went wrong. What if I panicked and froze and didn't know what to say to him. What if I said something and he didn't like it, didn't like me. What if I wasn't feeling well that day, what if I had a headache or a cold or I'd been so excited I hadn't slept for two days and could barely see straight. What if he was in a bad place, like when he went through his OxyContin phase or he'd just had a big row with Kim or his mum. What if I got there and to me it was this big big deal but to him I was just another blank face in a queue of nobodies and he wasn't really engaged. I'd tell him, I'd tell him what his music means to me how it helped me when I was feeling crap about myself but also how it gets the party started, gets conversations started (like this one), how he's so much more than just a dumb rapper he's made rap like literature like Shakespeare I actually started reading Shakespeare after listening to him. I'd want us to connect, him see a kindred spirit, give me his phone number or something but what if it didn't happen I'd be broken after flying all that way, it's just terrifying life you know that it's just completely fucking terrifying.

12. Teacher 1

Hello.

Hello.

Do you always spend lunch break in here?

I could ask you the same question.

Go on then.

What?

Ask.

Do you always spend your lunch break in my classroom.

If you're asking that question it means you don't normally.

But if you asked that question it means you don't normally.

Your logic is impeccable.

Ah well I spent a year studying logic.

What are you listening to?

Oh it's – one of those mixes.

I know this.

They're new I think.

It's really old, it was like last summer.

Ah.

So why are you in here?

Marking. One of the great joys of my existence. These are the moments we live for. The scratch of biro, the rustle of paper.

You know I could help you with that.

I'm not sure you've done this stuff.

No I mean I have a solution to your misery.

Oh yes?

Set less work.

Ha ha.

Why aren't you in the staffroom?

The staffroom's full of people moaning about their mortgages.

Oh.

Better not quote me on that. Why aren't you – wherever it is you normally spend your lunch break?

The hall's full of people moaning about their teachers.

Right.

Can I talk to you about something?

Of course. But don't shut the door. With just the two of us here. It's the rules.

Because they don't know what I might do to you

Something like that.

Can I change the track?

Okay.

Here.

Oh. Is this new?

It's The Beatles.

Oh. Yes. Of course.

I think my mum's having a nervous breakdown.

Your mum?

I think she's bulimic. I hear her vomiting. From my room. She thinks she's being quiet but. Last night I crept out into the hallway and stood outside the bathroom. I heard her. Just this little choking sound and then a sound like someone pouring chunky vegetable soup into a bowl of water

That's a very specific

...

I mean have you tried pouring chunky soup into a

No. You know.

I know. Sorry.

You've made me laugh. I'm telling you about my mum being sick and you

I'm sorry.

No it's good. So anyway I go back to my room and she flushes the toilet and the point is I come down half an hour later, it's like nearly midnight, she's on the sofa eating. Ice cream out the tub and marshmallows, she tries to hide the marshmallows under a cushion but I see it. So I know she isn't sick is that your daughter?

Yes.

She's cute.

Thank you.

…

It isn't necessarily bulimia. It could be stress. It could be a stomach condition that means she has an appetite even though she's being sick. It could be that she ate something funny. Or have you thought about the idea that she might be

She's not pregnant.

Right. I think the important thing is

Can I change the song?

Sure. I think the thing is, do you feel you want to talk to her about this?

Do you know these guys?

I grew up listening to this.

Really? You're older than I

Thanks.

Oh no I didn't mean

It's okay.

Did you ever see them live?

I did. Once.

What was it like?

Absolutely definitely one of the top-ten moments of my life.
They played this.

Oh my gosh.

Singing as desired.

Thanks for helping with my mum.

I'm not sure I

It's really good just to tell someone.

Well you know where to find me. If you need to –

I know where to find you.

13. Kiss Me 2 (The Objective)

There doesn't have to be a before or after just a moment where
two people connect, it doesn't have to be thought through it
doesn't have to be analysed there doesn't have to be a reason
it's just a beautiful point of connection between two humans,
it's the simplest thing it's wordless it doesn't matter about
language and words are all lies anyway aren't they the minute
you put something into words it isn't quite what you felt it's a
compromise it's watered down it's exaggerated it's approximate
it 'doesn't quite capture' but a kiss I mean by its very nature one
thing a kiss does is silence you and it doesn't have to be loaded
it doesn't have to lead to anything it's just you know there's
someone who did this study he's called Daniel something and
he calculated what our day is made of he reckons we experience
around twenty thousand individual moments every day

Are you filming this?

No.

Have you done this before?

No.

Did it work? Are you on drugs?

No and but so this would be just one just one moment among the nineteen thousand nine hundred and ninety-nine others you're going to have today.

But you've kind of killed the spontaneity by explaining it so much, haven't you?

14. A Spoonful of Cinnamon Powder (or Something Else Entirely)

Are you going to do it then?

I don't know.

Come on, try it.

I'm not sure.

Just once.

Why though? I mean what's the point?

It's just one of those things everyone has to do.

So you know what it's like

So you can say you've done it.

You don't want to die and say you never tried it.

I'm not going to die.

You might.

Have you really done it before?

Of course.

Try it.

Try it.

I don't

Don't be a scaredy

I'm not a

Come on then.

…So what do I

You just – close your eyes if you need to – and

No.

Why not?

Because.

That's not a reason.

Does it hurt?

No not really come on.

So what's the point?

It's just a thing.

It's fun it's, don't be so

Oh alright.

Okay?

Okay.

Okay.

Go on then.

Yes.

No. Wait, I

Come on. It's too late to change your mind.

15. Status Update

That moment when you realise you've written more status updates than actually said things out loud today? That.

16. The Decision

I just don't understand why I can't go.

I'm sorry this isn't open for discussion any more.

But other people my age are going.

Well you're not.

But WHY?

Because I said.

But you haven't given me a reason.

I'm really getting rather tired of this conversation.

So am I.

Good well then let's end it.

So I can go.

Absolutely not.

Well that's the only way this conversation is going to end, so

…

You just don't want me to grow up. You don't want me to have the experiences everyone else is having. You're actually stunting my growth by not letting me go, do you realise that? My emotional growth my person growth. Everyone else is going to have this experience and I'm not. It's all they'll talk about on Monday. They'll all be different, they'll be changed by it, and I'll be stuck behind. I'll be a retard, a cripple, a failure. I'll turn into the sort of person who has no friends and sits on their own at lunchtime and goes to the library and spends maths lessons drawing weird pictures of people being dead or with arms missing or plotting how to blow up the school yes I'll be that kid who gets guns and grenades and goes mental one day and goes into school with a backpack full of explosives and just starts shooting up everyone, kids teachers it doesn't matter because the whole world is fucked and then saves the final bullet for their own brains and then they find all these books and writings in his bedroom and also Nazi Swiss tikkas on the wall

Swastikas

And they trace it all to this moment where you stopped me developing the way other children are developing, stopped me socialising, stopped me gaining emotional intelligence and empathy through ex-curricular interactions with my peers and engagement in contemporary popular culture and instead consigned me to a life of solitude and video games. I'm going to go and play the most violent game I own where all you do is carjack and drive-bys and shooting grannies and puppies and I'm going to play the angriest music I can find, something I know you hate, and you're going to wish, wish, wish you'd let me go.

17. Days

Many more?

Fair few.

Joy

18. The Score

So how was it?

It was. It was. I mean how long have you got, I – … It was wonderful I suppose.

Good.

But I don't think I got everything right. I made a big mistake I think, quite early on. I had this incredible opportunity

Yes

(Well you know, I guess)… and well I could have taken it I should have taken it but I don't know I was holding out for something better I suppose or and or maybe I just wasn't ready for it or I was scared but. And I kept thinking – even straight after I was thinking – Is It Too Late To Change My Mind? And then at a certain point it seemed that definitely it was. But – see – that was the exact point at which I finally knew, I'd made the wrong – although, did I? Would it have been better if I'd…? I am actually asking.

I can't tell you, I'm afraid.

You can't

It's not how it works. I can only comment on what did happen.

Oh.

You did well. Largely.

I did?

You were often too harsh on yourself.

Huh…

Do you want to know your score?

You get a score?

It's something we took from computer games. It's still quite new.

Right

You don't have to know.

No, I think I do, I. Go on. Yes.

Okay. You scored eleven thousand, three hundred and sixty-one.

…Oh. Is that…? What's it out of?

We never really – we haven't agreed a limit.

What do other people get? Is there a ranking system or

We can't disclose any of that I'm afraid. Data protection. It's – don't get me started.

So. Eleven thousand

Three hundred and sixty-one.

It's

…

This doesn't feel like I expected it to feel like

What did you expect it to feel like?

I don't know. Do I still exist? Are you – ?

…

It's funny. So many things that seemed important… and now they're…

It was nice to meet you. It always is. And now I have to let you go. And you – have to let go. I enjoyed spending some time with you. I hope this was a nice moment for you too.

What happens now?

You get one last song.

I do?

For the journey. You get to choose it.

Oh god

I know.

I bet this takes some people ages.

Just concentrate on you.

I feel like I've met you before.

…

Okay. Do you know –

You don't need to say it.

Oh.

But the good news is we do have it.

So what now?

You go. Through here.

Wait. Can I have one last look? Please.

You can.

Singing as desired.

19. Pouring and Sipping

How long?

How long?

Since I mean, how long since

Since

Since you first

First

You first

Saw each other?

Come on.

Spoke?

No.

You mean

Since you first

…?

Connected.

Connected?

Since you knew (you're so annoying)

Since I knew

That you felt, or that you both

I don't think it was a specific moment.

Come on. Tell me.

Why?

I'm your

It was like pouring

With rain? (the day you)

Like pouring into a glass. A little bit at a time. And each time it was a nice feeling, a liquid feeling, then suddenly there's a point where you notice you have a full glass, well not full full but a glassful

I don't

And then you want to take a drink of it. Just a sip at first   ·
because you're not sure what the liquid is how strong it is what it might do to you but then you notice not only is it delicious and warm and smooth and also different every time actually but also every time you sip some more gets poured in and the more you sip the more gets poured, always a bit more than you sipped, and eventually you take bigger mouthfuls you gulp you guzzle you want to get to the bottom but no matter how much you drink the glass always ends up fuller than before (that's how it feels)

I don't know if I understand what you're

That's because it hasn't happened to you

Yet

Yet.

You don't know that though.

I do though.

How? What makes you think you know?

I can tell. Now that it's happened to me. I can tell. Your eyes don't your skin isn't

So how long

How long?

Since you first. 'Sipped'.

That would be telling.

20. In Point of Fact

Why are you lying like that?

I'm practising for my funeral.

21. Bungeeabseilskydive

Jump!

No!

Jump!

I can't!

Why not?

…

These people!

I KNOW!

But you said. You said you wanted to do something –

I thought I did! I wasn't thinking! This is the stupidest thing in
the world why would anyone want to

22. Better Belieber (Harry Me)

A pop star is visiting a hospital patient.

You know I'm so honoured that you asked me here. I mean
most people want to swim with dolphins right. Which actually
I've done and it's nowhere near as good as everyone says,
they're kind of slimy.

Do you know what I'd really like? Could you give us a moment
alone?

Is that

I don't think

Do I look like I'm about to rape him? I mean look at me.

I'm just a little conscious of time, we've got

It's fine. I'd like that.

Okay, well we've got a few minutes before the car

Can I interest you in a small lukewarm coffee? There's a
machine down the

Well put like that

Your hospital experience isn't complete without it.

Leaving.

So.

Okay now listen to me: I hate you. I hate this. I haven't listened
to you for like a year. No one I know likes you any more. I've
played along because my idiot father set this up through that
dufus meddling charity and I don't want him to feel like the
effort was wasted. I don't want to meet pop stars real or
manufactured. I don't want to skydive or swim with dolphins
which by the way is very distressing for the dolphin. I just want
to get better which given you're here I assume is officially Not
Going To Happen. And to have you turn up with your shiny
eyes and your perfect little life. Everything has gone so very
right for you and you have experienced so much amazing stuff
at such a young age and every day is scripted moment by
moment for your pleasure and convenience and we're all just
meant to live vicariously through the wild wild things you get to
do that we never will, the red carpet backstage parties Ferrari
jacuzzis and nothing could make me feel more bitter because in
the end it's the opposite of me. I won't get to do any of that
stuff because I'll be dead soon and even in the time I've had I
couldn't do most of the stuff you get to do because ONE I'm
not famous and TWO I've spent most of my life with tubes up
my nose and down my throat so I've never even had the chance
to try to be Anything kiss me. Kiss me or I'll tell everyone you
put your hand under the sheet tried to feel me up said you'd
flick that switch which is basically powering the stuff that's
keeping me alive if I didn't let you

…

More.

…

One thing. One thing now that I have on nearly everyone else
on the planet.

Returning.

Well.

Well.

How are we doing?

We're doing good.

It's been really nice to meet you. I'll pray for you.

I'll listen to your music.

Tweet me how you're doing.

I totally will.

Goodbye now.

Thank you so much.

Leaving.

Well. That was something. How was it?

It was really, really good.

So what did you talk about?

I asked him if he was really happy deep-down happy as one who'd expended his teenage years in the relentless pursuit of success in the field of entertainment, denied if magazines are to be believed all the normal stuff no privacy every move every mistake played out in public.

And

And he told me he hated it. He was pushed into it by his parents. Nothing he did was real. Nothing felt like his achievement. He said he hated every minute of his life. He said he'd swap places with me in an instant.

He said that

He said he sometimes wishes he could die.

23. Parenting

I had visions of you and me on the sofa. You sat crumpled, me
with one hand on your shoulder, a box of tissues in the other.
Being able to say with you, yes boys are idiots, and tell you all
the times my heart got broken. I pictured battles. Open warfare.
Doors slamming, pictures rattling on the wall, then slowly
working our way back into each other's trust and affection,
tearful making-up so we end up stronger than ever. I pictured the
speech you'd give at the surprise eighteenth birthday I'd throw
you – shortly before I slip away to a hotel so you can wreck the
house – where you acknowledge what a nightmare you've been
and pay tribute to me for being the voice of reason and
experience that guided you through the storm of adolescence into
the port of adulthood. God that's terrible, this is why I never
made it as a writer. I wanted to find drugs in your bedroom, make
a huge show of throwing them away then secretly retrieve them
from the rubbish bin and take them myself. Or maybe take them
with you. I wanted to hold you while you sicked up cider and
vodka, stroking you and scolding you at the same time. I wanted
you to lie to me as you stood chewing gum in the hallway that
you'd just been around people who were smoking and hadn't
yourself wouldn't dream of it and we both know you're lying
because I found a pack in your drawer when I was snooping
around your room last week. I wanted to read your diary and be
shocked at the horrible things you say about yourself. I wanted
just once for you to turn your music up too loud and for me to
genuinely hate what you listen to then dig out my old tapes and
debate whether anything would ever be as good. I wanted to
snoop your email your texts discover some dreadful secret – a
lover twice your age – or that someone had sent you a picture of
their penis, nothing else just their penis. I wanted you to go
through a phase of refusing to eat, then persuade you to love
yourself for who you are. I wanted a week where you wouldn't
even look at me. I wanted to go to your room at two in the
morning and find your bed empty and your window open. I
wanted to find scratches on your arms. I wanted you to wear
jumpers to hide the scratches on your arms, only I see them one
day when I walk in on you in the bath. I wanted you to run us out

of milk and butter and cereal and soap and never write them on the list. I wanted you to run out of condoms so I could lend you some. I wanted you to steal my favourite T-shirt, the one I wear when I want to pull. I wanted you to refuse to wear the coat I bought you last winter. I wanted you to come home with gauze over the stud in your eyebrow or the tattoo on your neck. I wanted to sit up late on my own drinking Scotch and worrying and be so relieved when you came home that I couldn't be angry. I wanted to hear you scream that life was impossible I was impossible that I'd never understand you, to laugh when you insisted I'd never felt the way you feel had no idea what it's like to be you. This is what I wanted. This is what my friends have. This is what I waited for, through all the dull dull years of teaching you to read and cross the road, wiping your bum and your snot, spooning you medicine, the thousand times I picked you up and dropped you off and listened to you drone on about your teachers and your schoolwork and your drama club and your insipid little friends. This is what you're denying me. I wish I'd had another child. There, I've said it. I wish I'd had another child and then you could have been the sensible grown-up older sibling. But you don't say anything. You just sit there. You sit there like a. Why won't you say anything?

24. Not Moving

Because you can't lie here for ever. Because sooner or later you have to get up. Because you will in fact feel better if you get up. Because you will feel better eventually. Because it's a beautiful day outside. Well okay not beautiful but the sun's definitely breaking through the – well it's stopped raining at any rate and later the temperature's – . Because lying there is just making it worse. And I'm not going to go away. I'm not going to leave you like this.

I wish you would. You should. Go and do the things you want to

No.

Go away.

No.

I feel like a sack of potatoes. I feel like a barrow of earth. I feel
like an industrial-strength bag of garden rubble, all the pebbles
and twigs bashing into each other inside me and loose dusty soil
clogging up my lungs nose mouth every pore of my skin. I feel
like I have leaking sandbags over my eyes. I feel like twenty-
seven caterpillars have crawled through my ears into my skull
and made cocoons in the folds of my brain, so everything's
muffled and nothing can get anywhere there's just traffic and
congestion and my thoughts getting lost among all the cocoons
and eventually they're going to hatch into moths a hundred
moths fluttering about inside my head and that will be the point
when, that will be the point when – . I feel like my skin is made
of tree bark. I feel like crying for hours but I feel like all my
tears have dried up leaving only salt. I'm made of salt. I feel
like I've forgotten how to walk.

Moths?

Yes.

Not butterflies

…

I could order pizza?

Okay.

Okay?

Okay. Can we have pepperoni?

Of course. A pizza without pepperoni is like a bird without
wings. Where's the

It's in the

I'll go and

No. No because you won't know where it – I'll get it. Wait. I'll
get it.

25. Teacher 2 (We Have to Go)

Do you have to go?

Soon.

I wish you didn't.

I know. Me too. I just want to be with you.

Same. Same.

We should go away together. Don't you think?

That would be

Just the two of us. Somewhere no one knows us.

Where would you want to go?

Where would you want to go?

Have you ever been to Paris?

Yes.

Did you like it?

I don't really remember. I was six.

Or what about New York

…

Or Barcelona, that's an amazing

I don't want to go somewhere that's just full of stuff to look at where it's all statues and tour buses or and all you do is just spend the whole time eating and drinking and lying about. You can do that here. I want to go somewhere horrible.

Right

Somewhere life is completely shit. Where people don't have all the stuff we have. Where they're suffering. Where we can help them. Because I think we'd be awesome at that. Don't you?

No, I, totally. You're right. You're absolutely, that's

Do you want to go somewhere with me and help people?

Yes I do yes.

Okay. Look at this.

...

These girls right. They're ten, twelve years old. Every day,
twice a day, they walk four miles to the lake to fill their
jerrycans with water that isn't even clean I mean the people
who live close to the lake – look, here, see – they throw their
toilet waste into it, they drive diesel motorboats and then there's
these industrial plants no one knows what they're pumping in.
So then these girls walk all the way back with this huge weight
of dirty water balanced on their head and then at dusk they do
the same thing all over again. Along dirt tracks through bushes
and scrubland and they're vulnerable, they have no way to
defend themselves. And there are these fishermen who don't
live any one place they travel from one section of the lake – it's
a really big lake it's the size of a country – from one section to
another so no one knows them no one recognises them and they
prey on these girls, they wait in the bushes behind a tree for one
or two travelling alone when no one's around and they drag the
girls into the scrub and rape them

That's

But then if all this isn't enough the girls can't come home
without the jerrycans filled with water, they'll be told off no one
will believe their story or they don't dare tell because it brings
shame on the family, people assume they must have flirted with
the men, provoked them, and so having been raped and their
jerrycans, which never seem to have lids, knocked to the ground
and the water spilled everywhere they have to pick themselves
up brush off the dirt and twigs and insects and shit, clean their
bodies as best they can then walk back to the lake risk running
into their attackers again fill up the jerrycans again and carry
them all the way home as fast as they – weak with pain –
everything hurting knowing they'll be scolded for dawdling I
mean can you

It's terrible. It's. But I mean

So you can go out there. All you have to do is fly into the capital, look, then it's like eleven hours by bus but the point is you can go to where they are and there's this camp and they need, they need labour they need diggers and and bricklayers and but it's just basic skills you're just building wells, water wells, inside each village so none of them have to go to the lake, they can go to school instead they can grow up and become something because these girls they can't get an education so they have no skills so they can't leave the village so they're just married off, as soon as they, as soon as they, I mean if they're not pregnant from rape they're pregnant from marriage by thirteen, fourteen but if they didn't have to walk they'd have time to learn things and they could leave and become something not exist solely to be pumped full of sperm and spit out more kids into this this misery of a

Wow you really

So what do you think?

Well we should do it. I mean of course. I mean next summer maybe if

I don't see how anyone with a heart could not want to do this. Not once they realise what's actually happening.

Well no I agree.

And the thing is life's so cheap out there and you can live in a tent because it's so warm and eat for like nothing compared to what it costs here so it doesn't matter about money even

You've got such a good heart, you're so – I

So I stole my mum's credit card.

You

It's the one she doesn't use, she won't notice for – and I found my passport. There's a flight that leaves in four hours, it has seats I checked, so if we book now then go straight to the airport

I love it, you just, you're like

I'll leave a message that I'm at Sam's or Alex's.

Brilliant

You really don't need to pack much.

No, I

When we get there we'll probably need to dye our hair or shave it or something. Because people will probably be looking for us but we can get all that at the airport. You can get malaria tablets out there they're actually cheaper and um that's it, everything I need's in here.

…

So come on. We need to book the

You're not. You're not joking. Are you? I mean it's the middle of. You know and we both have – on Monday morning – we both have

But what does that matter? Really? Compared to this. Compared to us.

26. Leading Question

What do you think about euthanasia?

27. Not Working

What would you have been?

I'd have been President of America. It's definitely the best job.

But don't you have to be born there?

They'd make an exception. They made an exception for Obama didn't they?

Did they?

Because he's such a great guy.

You could be Prime Minister of Britain.

That's a bit boring.

Or President of France, then you'd get loads of cheese.

Mmm cheese

Or President of Germany

I think it's called Chancellor

Chancellor of Germany then you'd get loads of – what do they have in Germany?

I don't know.

German cheese!

Mmm cheese

But still and so also

Yes?

You haven't really said

What's wrong with being this?

No but come on I mean

I don't know. A doctor maybe a teacher. But then also not because I think I always knew I wouldn't.

28. On the Phone

It's just after midnight and I'm standing at the end of the platform at the train station. And this is the last thing I'll, these are the last words I'm ever going to say. I hope you can see me, there isn't much light this far down but it's the only place away from the cameras, well apart from this camera, but. I mean this is the new one it's meant to have enhanced night-vision recording or something. Probably a bit of a waste, with hindsight, getting a new phone, but my contract was due for renewal and to be honest I just wanted to know what it was like. Which is actually pretty depressingly similar to the old one once the novelty of a few new features has worn off why am I even talking about this? Anyway it's quiet so at least hopefully you can... It's quite nice here actually. Quite peaceful. There you go. Like I say it's just after midnight so the last train's gone and now it's just the fast trains that pass through here on the way back to the city. And I do feel bad. For the person driving the train and the people on it, some of them anyway, the ones I'd have liked, and the police and ambulance and whoever it is that has to – (*The sound of an approaching train.*) That's a. It's early. Or the one before's late. It must be the one before because they're never early. I mean I worked this out, this is pretty premeditated, I don't know if that helps but... but I haven't said what I want to say. Look I'll have to stop a moment to let it pass. Because it will be too loud to – (*The sound of the train passing.*) Quite exhilarating actually. Standing this close. The sound and the speed. The way it pushes air into your face... So I'm leaving this phone as well as my wallet which contains identification. Here on the platform next to where I... And now I'm going to explain why I've made this decision. Why I don't feel I can carry on with... Someone. Someone I went to see, and they. Told me to make lists. Things that are wrong and things that I'm grateful for. And I'm sure it's a good technique for some people but... One. I don't – I can't – I'm sick, basically, and I don't think I'm going to get better. And the world is so. I mean at any given moment millions of people are suffering, really actively suffering, starving and ill and being burnt and scarred, and we all just carry on, we know what's happening but we ignore it, we occupy ourselves with trivial little problems, and then – then we go on about living good lives and everyone's just so selfish, if you stop and think about it it's sickening and once you realise that how can any of us live with ourselves?

Give me your phone.

What?

I need your phone. Give it to me.

No.

This is actually a mugging, I am mugging you.

Have you a got a weapon?

I'm strong. I can hurt you. I'll. I'll push you in front of a

You can't take my phone.

I have to. You don't understand. I have to.

You can – you can have some money if you'll go away.

It has to be the phone.

I need this phone.

I need it more.

You don't seem like a mugger to me.

…

Look, just go. I won't tell anyone I won't call the police this never happened.

No. I need that phone. I'm really sorry. But when I set my mind on doing something I make a point of never going back.

Alright. I'm leaving.

No.

Get out of my way.

Give me the phone.

NO.

A struggle. Two people who can't win. Then, the sound of a train.

...

Look out!

Train passes.

...

Fuck it. Have it.

Are you sure?

Just – let me delete something.

Okay. I actually quite enjoyed fighting with you. We're quite evenly matched.

Here.

Thanks. Are you – is this really okay?

What don't you want it any more?

Well I didn't really win it.

I'm letting you have it because I don't want to fight you any more. Is that enough of a victory for you?

Does it hurt?

Everything hurts.

Me too. What were you doing here? I mean the last train's gone. I saw you come here. I was – kind of following you. I could probably give you this phone back in a day or two. I only need it for – If you give me your number I'll – oh. I mean not your number. But. Your email address? Or are you on Face– no maybe not Facebook. Or I could post it, if you

...

I guess I'll figure out who you are from this. I'll try to get this back to you maybe like Monday evening? Would that be okay? Look. I mean. Thank you. Um, my life's pretty – this was really. It's hard to explain. This was really important to me.

Leaving.

Nothing. Nothing. Nothing goes right for me. (*Consulting something.*) Leaves midnight-oh-six. Four minutes, seven minutes, two minutes, midnight nineteen. Fuck it. Fuck it. Fuck it.

Returning.

Hi excuse me. You had a missed call and I just thought – It said Mum and I wondered if it would be important. Given how late it is. Also what are you actually doing here? You're not a trainspotter are you. You don't look like a – and you don't have a – were you using this (*Phone.*) to record the – But then why would you still be here. Oh wait were you going to – were you going to. Oh my god. Wait no, stay, stay. You need your. Hang on I'm calling your mum back. This is going to be hard to explain.

…

(*Into phone.*) Hello no this is someone else but Sam is here but. (*Away from phone.*) Hi Sam. (*Into phone.*) Oh. Oh. Look, I don't really know Sam. But to me he seems like a good person, a good – and he fights well and – yeah hang on wait. The point is I think right now he really does need to speak to you and for you to – I think he needs to hear how much you love him. Can you do that? And then make sure he gives the phone back to me when he's done that's quite important too.

29. Refrain

Tip. Fill. Carry. Pour.

Tip. Fill. Carry. Pour.

Tip. Fill. Carry. Pour.

Tip. Fill. Carry. Pour.

Fall.

30. Terms and Conditions

Sign here.

Thank you.

I just need to read you the terms and conditions.

Okay.

You agree that your use of this service is at your own risk. You are supplied as-is and may not be refunded or exchanged.

Okay.

Your body or vessel is licensed to you for the duration of its lifespan but remains ultimate property of Living Vessels Incorporated brackets LVI. LVI does not guarantee represent or warrant that use of your vessel will be free from error loss corruption attack viruses interferences or other intrusion and is indemnified from any liability relating hereto.

Okay.

Living Vessels Incorporated further indemnifies itself from any direct, indirect, incidental, punitive, special or consequential damages arising to others from your use of its service.

Okay.

LVI retains the rights to all images, ideas and experiences invented or acquired by you in your use of its service, for promotional purposes on our own networks, including potentially but not limited to your first steps your first words your first day at school your first kiss your first funeral your first broken arm your first broken heart your first-class degree and your first-degree burns.

…Okay.

Your battery life is limited and will begin to deplete from the moment you begin. No guarantees are undertaken regarding the lifespan of your battery. Battery life varies between models, consult literature, art, music, philosophy or the medical profession for more information.

Okay.

This is you, the essence of you, in your purest state. You begin
in a cell, then grow like mould in the womb of a lady who for
your whole life you will alternately worship and revile. You will
be squeezed from her body, your head compressed as in a
clamp, a trauma neither of you will allow the other to forget.
You will stare with glassy eyes, grab at things, wail to express
your instant disappointments, which you will expect instantly to
be resolved. You'll have a birthday every year. Some people
will die before you. You'll build memories, assets, a personal
narrative, things you consider achievements, things you
consider regrets. You may eventually adopt, or at least emulate,
my role. Finally you will find out the answer to one of the only
true mysteries of the human experience.

Which is?

What death feels like.

Oh.

Any questions?

I do, I think.

Go on.

All those things you mentioned. They sound like they're going
to happen whether I want them to or not.

I think that's largely correct.

So what can I actually do?

You mean, what can you choose to do that's different to what
everyone else is doing?

I suppose so.

Pretty much whatever you like, within the boundaries of the
natural laws of the universe and to a lesser extent the laws,
customs and freedoms of the state you're in.

I'm just – can you give me something specific?

You can dance.

Dance

You can repair damage to other people's vessels.

Repair. I'm still not

You can pour tubs of ice-cold water over yourself if that's what you really want to do.

Ice-cold – but why would

People spend their days doing all manner of strange things. They sit in darkened rooms for hours staring at images that will surprise you – you who are still an empty page. They inflict suffering instead of picking fruit. They poison themselves, sometimes just with thoughts. They do things they know will shorten their lives yet all the while bemoan their lack of time. They use their life to plan their demise. They attempt the ultimate futile action – to steal the battery life of another vessel, or, if they can't steal it, to corrupt and so shorten it so that theirs seems better by comparison. Some people will try to drink from your glass. Some, to fill it. Approach both with caution. And please note that you can convince yourself of anything.

That's a lot to think about.

You'll forget it all in a moment. But at at some level, you'll always know it. So. Are you ready?

Wait, there's something

Yes?

About the battery life.

Ah.

Does it say how long mine is?

No.

Can you tell me?

Of course. Most people don't want to know, but I'm happy to tell you.

Maybe I'm different to most people.

Most people think that. It's not always a good thing.

Being different? Or thinking it?

Being smart. So, your battery life… Oh.

What? What?

You're sure you want to know

Why? Is it really short?

Suppose it was shorter than average. If I told you, you'd go through life desperate to make each moment count. You'd always say yes. You'd be fearless, in a way, knowing that nothing could hurt you until the point that everything did. Where others dawdled and slumped you'd be upright and striving. For you there'd never be a later, a next time, a second –

It sounds great

It sounds physically exhausting and emotionally draining.

I think. I think I could handle it. Knowing the truth. I think maybe it's better to know than just stumble on in ignorance.

Ah. But. Suppose your battery life turns out not to be so short. Suppose it turns out to be unusually long. Where would you find the motivation, knowing there will always be time to try again? Knowing that everyone you ever love will die before you. Your reward for longevity is the greatest suffering imaginable – witnessing the slow decay of everyone else. Or suppose your battery life is merely average – whatever average happens to be for your era, state and social milieu. How will you feel going through life trapped inside a vessel that you have come to realise, so early on, is nothing more than mediocre? How could you dance? How could you repair other vessels? How could you soar?

I see.

But, if you want to know, I will tell you. It's up to you.

It's up to me.

It's your decision. It has be.

Okay.

Okay?

Okay.

Right. Well, your battery life is

No. Don't tell me. Sorry. I don't want to know. Sorry.

Fine. It's a shame, actually.

Oh?

But there's a useful lesson here: you always have the right to change your mind.

Oh. Okay. Well maybe I… no. I definitely don't want to know.

So it turns out, under scrutiny, that you are like most people.

Oh.

For many, that realisation comes as something of a relief.

So what now?

If you accept these terms and conditions please sign here. If you do not accept these terms and conditions please do not sign here and please do not use this service.

Okay. I accept.

Right here. Thank you.

Is that it? Does it start now?

It's already started. Several minutes have elapsed in fact. It began with your first signature. This one.

Oh. Oh. I didn't realise. I. I've just wasted the first part of my life.

Time takes some getting used to.

What did I miss?

Not much. Just your conception

Oh, but that would have been

One way or another, everyone seems to miss it.

Oh.

The awful thing is when people decide not to sign the second line – to reject our terms. Then we have to – conclude – something that's already begun. That always seems to cause a lot of heartache.

Oh. So where do I go?

In here. You get to float for a while in warmth, with all your food and drink brought to you. Enjoy it. Once it's over, you'll mainly only do this for two or three weeks in a year. It was nice to meet you. We don't often get people so young.

What. What does that mean?

Oh nothing. It's just that – when you're here, you present yourself as you will be at the exact point in time at which you consider yourself most entirely *you*. Maybe the point at which you are happiest, or strongest, or most fulfilled. It's always interesting to see. That's all. Enjoy your vessel and thank you for using LVI.

Wait no you still haven't told me – I still don't get – I mean what do I actually *do*, what am I trying to achieve, what's the objective, how do I know if I've

31. So Happy I Could Cry

You look so sad.

I feel sad.

But you were happy a second ago. You said. You said you were really happy.

I still am. But I'm so happy I'm sad. Because when I'm this happy I know this is the happiest I can feel. And I know this moment isn't going to last for ever even though I want it to. And I'm only going to feel less happy afterwards. And even recognising the fact that I'm happy, and thinking about the fact that the moment isn't going to last, is making me less happy. Because I've already ruined it, just by thinking about it.

Do you like Chinese food? Do you like statues? There's this… Do you want to go out with me?

32. Kiss Me 3 (The Goal)

It's just a question of which experiences you want to have.

Which experiences I want to

If you have this experience, if you actually do this, it will become a memory and you'll have that memory for the rest of your life. You'll carry it with you like a favourite teddy bear, a blanket, a photograph you never throw away. If you don't do this, you won't have the experience. It won't be inside you. Only the memory of not doing it, of running away, your imagination of what it might have been like which is always going to fall short on specifics and finally the question what might have been.

But you're assuming I'll like the experience you're assuming I'll want the memory.

You don't have to like the experience I mean I think you will I hope you will but you don't have to. You just have to live it and then later it will be there for you to reflect on to draw on, it will mean different things at different points in your life.

But what if I hate the experience? What if it scars me? What if I go through life wishing I'd never done it?

Do you really think all that can come out of one kiss?

I don't know. I don't know. I need to think about it.

Okay. Although actually you don't because

Will you just let me think about it?

Okay.

…Okay I've thought about it.

You've thought about it?

Yes.

And?

Okay.

Okay?

Yes.

Now?

Now.

…

Okay?

Okay.

33. The End

Is this it?

I think so. Yes.

I don't know what to say. I thought I would, when the time came. And I knew it would come. But now we're here and I don't know what to say.

You don't have to say anything.

No. But

We could sing?

Sing

Singing as desired.

Are you ready?

Yes. Okay. Now.

End of play.

A Nick Hern Book

buckets first published in Great Britain in 2015 as a paperback original by Nick Hern Books Limited, The Glasshouse, 49a Goldhawk Road, London W12 8QP, in association with the Orange Tree Theatre

buckets copyright © 2015 Adam Barnard

Adam Barnard has asserted his right to be identified as the author of this work

Cover image: Getty Images

Designed and typeset by Nick Hern Books, London
Printed and bound in Great Britain by Mimeo Ltd, Huntingdon, Cambridgeshire PE29 6XX

A CIP catalogue record for this book is available from the British Library

ISBN 978 1 84842 492 0

www.nickhernbooks.co.uk

facebook.com/nickhernbooks

twitter.com/nickhernbooks